SCRIBNER
POETRY

ALSO BY MATTHEW ZAPRUDER

I LOVE HEARING YOUR DREAMS

POEMS

MATTHEW ZAPRUDER

SCRIBNER

NEW YORK   LONDON   TORONTO   SYDNEY   NEW DELHI

Scribner
An Imprint of Simon & Schuster, LLC
1230 Avenue of the Americas
New York, NY 10020

First Scribner hardcover edition September 2024

SCRIBNER and design are trademarks of Simon & Schuster, LLC

Simon & Schuster: Celebrating 100 Years of Publishing in 2024

For information about special discounts for bulk purchases, please contact Simon &
Schuster Special Sales at 1-866-506-1949 or business@simonandschuster.com.

The Simon & Schuster Speakers Bureau can bring authors to your live event. For
more information or to book an event, contact the Simon & Schuster Speakers
Bureau at 1-866-248-3049 or visit our website at www.simonspeakers.com.

Interior design by Kathryn A. Kenney-Peterson

Manufactured in the United States of America

10 9 8 7 6 5 4 3 2 1

Library of Congress Cataloging-in-Publication Data

Names: Zapruder, Matthew, 1967– author.
Title: I love hearing your dreams : poems / Matthew Zapruder.
Description: First edition. | New York : Scribner, 2024.
Identifiers: LCCN 2024015328 (print) | LCCN 2024015329 (ebook) | ISBN
    9781668059807 (hardcover) | ISBN 9781668059814 (paperback) | ISBN
    9781668059821 (ebook)
Subjects: LCGFT: Poetry.
Classification: LCC PS3626.A67 I46 2024 (print) | LCC PS3626.A67 (ebook)
    | DDC 811/.6—dc23/eng/20240404
LC record available at https://lccn.loc.gov/2024015328
LC ebook record available at https://lccn.loc.gov/2024015329

ISBN 978-1-6680-5980-7
ISBN 978-1-6680-5982-1 (ebook)

for Sarah and Simon, always

CONTENTS

I LOVE
HEARING
YOUR
DREAMS

I LOVE HEARING YOUR DREAMS

like those poems
I write in my sleep
and forget

the ones
that babble
some essential message

to the trees
I can only
walk toward

in that particular
dark I see
when I turn

away from the world
returning
I always

forget my best work
like those forgotten
poems your dreams

have no hidden
agenda to be wise
they are made

to be forgotten
so something
can be known

tonight I was woken
by a light passing
along our shade

I heard you cry out
you would not stop
until I gently

shook you
your eyes
in the ordinary light

through the window
were still yours
yet you wore

a distant face
not like
a mask at all

before you spoke
your face became
a son an animal

a chair
you looked as if
you just discovered

you were holding
keys to a lake
you could still

hear your parents
laughing they were
not yet married

on your face things
kept turning
into each other

pages left
in the wind
then I heard you

say it was
the strangest thing

IT WAS SUMMER. THE WIND BLEW

It was summer. The wind blew
away from me, and I stayed here thinking
about a certain mountain. Things got green
then forgot, and in their forgetting
remembered everything that was not
grass, or me. My son forgot
he could not swim, then emerged
tall as laughter, hidden
as the lesson in a song. He forgot
how to tie his shoes then
learned how to draw a face
and tie it to a string and run far off
into the place only he could go.
I chased him but he just grew larger.
For a week he became a carpenter,
hammering filled my heart. My heart
went to the hardware store and bought
all the napping spatulas. It was
summer, so I let them stay up
all night, or they let me.
We swung from the magnolia,
our great leaves fell, it remained
our friend. Each day was that same
sweet holiday that never ended
until the windows got soft. It was summer.
Candles came on like televisions.
That was the last time things were real.

MY GRANDMOTHER'S DICTIONARY

It must have arrived in the hands
of a salesman whose name
shall remain unrecorded. Let's
call him the handsome stranger.
She saw him through the little
window next to the door
and knew although she did not
believe she believed in such
things she had loved him
in a former life. She gave him
a glass of her legendary tea
and let him go. My grandfather
was upstairs in the immaculate
attic where after they died
I found this typewriter
sleeping among old blueprints.
During the war he diagrammed
routes so trucks of soldiers
could arrive precisely in time
to wait for their orders. Or
he worked in parts. I don't
remember. I can only picture
that afternoon he told me
exactly who he had been,
I hear the resigned
tone but not what he said,
I was as is my nature staring
out the kitchen window
thinking some great hypothesis

that could easily be disproved,
that day now lost in the book
no one can ever turn
around and read. This was
in a little town that was a harbor,
its restaurant a windmill
replica turning in no wind.
We never asked her why she
always stood in the darkest
part of any room. Once
she looked up from her
eternal soup long enough to say
to me, you really must remove
that terrible beard. What
is the name of that sort
of love? I want to look it up,
I think it comes from the Latin
for not knowing the Greek
for the particular quiet
of that afternoon I finally
gave in and picked up
the forbidden ceramic lion
from the shelf, it slipped
from my hands that already
trembled as they do today
and hit the very thick carpet
with a silent thud, exploding
into so many tiny pieces.
Out of the kitchen she came
with a broom and we both
pretended it was never there.
What is that sort of love?

The dictionary knows. I opened
it and found dust. I remember
it had a solitary gold stripe
across blue-grey fabric like a dress
you wear only once, by the sea.

THOUGHTS ON PUNCTUATION

Staple the ghost to the page
with your favorite symbol
and you might find out too much
or end up prosecuting
wind for lack of commitment
when it blows the clouds around
describe the wind with precision
torture it for a while
it will tell you what you know
sometimes I see the future
is just the past in a suit
that will never be in style
it wears your father's trilby
shadowing a face that answers
you with a semicolon
linking unrelated facts
like a modern oracle
a conglomerate employs
when I rattle on like this
saying useless things are true
such as the Egyptians used marks
shaped like cats to divide words
please slap me with a hyphen
put me back on the shelf
next to that old wooden game
it had complicated rules
for diagramming our thoughts
about who we should become
so we could leave them behind
we played it one whole winter

so deeply absorbed we died
then were reborn as commas
happy to go on and on

TWO SLEEPS
for Mary Ruefle

When the other father
told his child
something will happen
in two sleeps
at first I didn't understand
he meant something
comforting, time
passing with quick
ease, a way
to measure nights
numbered in unearned
peace. I just thought
of my own two sleepers,
who often wake,
waking me though
even in sleep
I am always
already awake
at that oddest hour
that does not end,
the crooked, unnumbered one.
Then they fall back
into their respective
oblivions. I lie
shrouded in this barge
that does not cross
the river, listening. No
music of the dead,
no wise silence,

no penultimate dream.
I just worry every particle
can now be counted,
that we are all caretakers
of a dying patient
named the self,
or the sea.
I lie here and worry
I am worrying about
all the wrong things
according to some system
I worry I myself created,
probably in my sleep.
It is very utterly dark.
Like a branch in total
darkness I cannot
be discerned. All night
I stand beneath the tree.

BAD BEAR

if you see one
you can say
bad bear
right to its face
even if you're not sure,
maybe it's good
and has discretion
in relation
to the delicious
treasury of human
garbage or even
the eternal
work of bees,
who knows,
but it's ok
on the path
with your thunder voice
unequivocally
to condemn it,
lore says that
will make it leave
so you can go
tell your story
in the tent
and again at the table
laughing without asking
what violence
brought you there,
you and all
that food

from everywhere,
those flowers
you eat
and do not wonder
who told you
it's ok to lie
even to the rich
or to save a life
even your own,
in the middle of night
in the cave
you will hear
the eternal question
even darker
than what surrounds,
was I born this way
or was it circumstance
that condemned me,
silence answers
you were born
to be condemned
everywhere
but in poems,
for a while you hang
dead leaves
on the night tree
then they fall away
and all that is left
is this honey
you stole from the world

DEAD FLOWERS
for Gerald Stern

now that you are gone
I'll never get hit

by a piano dropped from a cloud
I'll probably die

holding a book I told
everyone that I read

without you everything will be the same
my son turns his light on so early

I have already thought unspeakable thoughts
and you will never drive again

along some river with too many
consonants in its name

it will keep flowing
north like the Nile

crying tears of comprehending joy
without irony or shame

it is said you were always talking
about how good you were at dancing

and it is said you wore
a hat made of straw that you stole

from the perfectly preserved
room of a dead poet

it is said you said
he didn't need it anymore

I told my friend I was going to write you
in the hospital but as is my way

I keep learning if you don't write it down
the thought just flies away

where does it go
maybe into the trees

or someone else's head
and isn't that the point anyway

now that you are gone
I can say to every pigeon I pass

that it was beautiful to be a nun
having unspeakable thoughts

and you will not hear me
or maybe who knows

I remember going to your door
on the wrong evening with a friend

I see no longer
the party was next weekend

we listened to dead flowers
all the way back to Boston in shame

now that you are gone
I can finally write this poem

I can say the only true thing
I remember going to your door

TELL ME WHY

who can tell me
the names of those flowers

I know I've been informed
a thousand times

by you kind stranger
before you are finished

I'm already forgetting
it's not you

kind one my flower
ignorance is eternal

and last night the meadow
was busy

having private thoughts
today the mourners

are praising their dead
walking apart

from us their heads
bowed in black conundrum

tomorrow they will dissolve
back into the rest of us

the names of the flowers
I love most

leave me
as soon as they arrive

and my soul
is a little lighter

that meadow
remembers

but cannot say
I asked my mentor

the mountain
but she is dead

though she is not
she just knows

I won't listen
when I ask where to go

I keep asking
what are their names

with them
I cannot be trusted

if I could only remember
them I would stop

writing *tomorrow*
in the book of dreams

THE LOCKSMITH

You used to be able to see the mountain
from the front window of our store
and the railroad track that went north
the train stopped not too far from here
and dropped off people who wanted to place
their tired bodies in the medicinal waters
the train went on to the timberlands
disappearing into the fog
now all you can see are buildings
and everything is covered over
no one even knows there used to be
a spring with minerals that healed
the body's mysterious pains
it still runs under the alley
you can hear it at night
in the shop no one can easily find
a lot of things aren't useful anymore
but it seems locks will always be
just complicated enough
we used to bevel the keys by hand
but it's still an art to use this machine
I hope to die here in this little room
just like my grandfather who said
here's your receipt but don't worry
even though everything has changed
no one has ever returned with a key
I carved to open what opens not

POEM FOR RUPI KAUR

Lying in bed at 3 a.m.
listening to him cough
in his bear pajamas
is not fun
there is no joy
right now
or ever now
that I know
my heart lives
outside my body
in him and the grass
and my wife
because you wrote
defeated eyes
I know you understand
how I feel
when I say
the high fever of night
there are no defenses
again I do the math
will I live long enough
to see him thrive
in what sort of world
we are living
not in but on
you know what I mean
one of the continents
is on fire
you are not
wrong to think

in poems
we can solve
something complicated
a lot of things
are not *information*
here in the middle
of complicated night
it has become clear
we cannot trust
the central metaphor
which is we are children
though it is true
we are not
safe anywhere
I love my son
his little bear pajamas
my wife the grass
the ends of poems

PEORIA

I don't know when that name
entered my ear. I remember
hearing that was where
my father won his first case.
He must have stayed a while,
maybe in the Mark Twain Hotel.
He could not have been far
from young Richard Pryor.
Maybe the famous
brown bison watched him
from a field or a commemorative
mug with facts about megafauna
and the Quaternary extinction
event on the other side.
A few still live in the zoo,
their shaggy mountainous
shoulders permanently
hunched in preemptive defeat.
Years of constant travel.
Whenever he returned
from whatever city
he would bring a snow globe
back for her. You could
turn or shake it and see
white flakes far too slowly
descend through some
eternally clear liquid onto
appropriate plastic landmarks.
Among them people stilled
in the act of moving agree

life is elsewhere and the past
always misremembered,
so they shall stay forever
here and be loved. O happy
shadows of the ordinary.
A collection of plastic
half eggs translucently
covering various midsize cities
cherished on a mantel grew.
I don't remember seeing
Peoria, maybe that was before
the first time he had almost
not remembered
and with guilty gratitude
stuck the far too expensive
trinket in the pocket
of his overcoat, running
to the plane soon to be filled
with that once ubiquitous smoke.
It flew through years
of undefeated night
toward our capital.
I had not yet been born.
Here I've been slowly learning
to speak to these nameless
purple flowers in their language,
in which Peoria means
mountainside hidden
in productive shade
between orchard and dream.
It's where they grow. I see
the planets glowing

on a wall above my own son's bed.
The past is always misremembered.
Hold it to your ear. It has
the sweet hum of the superstore
buried inside an apple. You can
almost hear it say be glad
your father never told you
elsewhere, that's where life is.

JURY DUTY

I wanted to waste the day
not making lists
refusing to watch
the final episode
of democracy on a screen
attached to a mysterious
silver box issued
by an institution
whose proboscis I willingly
inserted into my soul
so I can produce these
endless translucent complaints
O whoever you are
out there laughing
on the street I will
give you my name
which has in these long
hours grown less
precious than a shadow
take it and go
forth without my confusion
I do not know
which candidates
won't dress us
in uniforms
though it is true it would
be one fewer decision
no more staring
into the endless
darkness of the closet

with its bulb that burned out
a thousand years ago
where did I put my headlamp
I last saw it in a drawer
poured in the final
frantic moments into
a box no one labeled
stuff that will be utterly
vital only once
we moved onto
this hill and I no
longer can find
anything not useful
I like to stare
in the mirror
and see an explorer
who convinced the king
of maps to let him
sail off the edge
leaving me here
to doze on the couch
until the bus summons
me with its hiss
I have at last been called
I finally feel ready
to ignore all the evidence
I put on my robes
powder my wig
step into my long
pointed shoes and go
holding my unforgiving
gavel into the innocent world

POEM FOR JEAN FOLLAIN

When I read
your poems I feel
I will never
be able to return
to the dark forest
of Saint-Lô
I will never go
to your grave at the mouth
of a tunnel where laughing
flowers suggestively
draped think
it's good you never
learned to speak
any language
but their own
they think only
they can hear
you say
true revolution
begins with music
I hold your
book and listen
for further instructions
can you tell me
what should I do
with these cassette tapes
and my old terror
of the ordinary
yes it's true
all day everyone

drowns for lack
of manifested
dreams but
I still can't say
I believe in revolution
I can't forget
in our language
it still means
a return
to eternal ruins
with your echo
I agree
to make the new
we need
to think for a long
time about
the little windows
singing
in the blue door
though sometimes
it is true the urge
for wilder colors
on the ends of flagpoles
arrives to me
in the forlorn hammock
where I hear
myself say
wake me please
is the revolution here
its wild colors

KING OAK

O take my upper branches
like the Romans did
from the top of me

make some space
for sunlight to get in

little emerald bugs
can bring their glittering thoughts

I promise to never share them

I have lived so many hundred years
next to the castle
in fear of the Tree Council

each year they vote to let me
watch the children come at night
and carve the same names
into my torso

then play in the canopy
of my hair

if one of my branches falls
pick it up soon or the King will die

burn it deep in the forest

sing to the green moss

OF HORACE

I could sit here all night
until I fall asleep
in this chair I inherited
from my father's office
where I would for hours
listen to him talk
to Los Angeles or Korea
entranced as he crafted
tensile sentences
out of the air
until every plan
had the cobalt gleam
of honed practicality
his clients adored him
he was tall and dignified
his limbs draped
inside suits handmade
by a man he took me
once to visit
we stood together
in a narrow room
I was not yet tall
I watched them talk
in low tones
then out into the sunlight
we emerged together
I knew there was something
I should have learned
but all I remember
is the tailor's name

Mr. D'Orazio
which means
Of Horace
that is belonging
to the poet of odes
celebrating common things
not Golden Son

POEM FOR A SUICIDE

The yellow flowers on the grave
make an arch, they lie

on a black stone that lies on the ground
like a black door that will always

remain closed down into the earth,
into it is etched the name

of a great poet who believed
he had nothing more to say,

he threw himself into literal water
and everyone has done their mourning

and been mourned over, and we all
went on with our shopping,

I stare at this photograph of that grave
and think you died like him,

like all the others,
and the yellow flowers

seem angry, they seem to want
to refuse to be placed

anywhere but in a vase
next to the living, someday

all of us will have our names
etched where we cannot read them,

she who sealed her envelopes
full of poems about doubt

with flowers called it her
"granite lip," I want mine

to say Lucky Life, and what would
a perfect elegy do? place the flowers

back in the ground? take me
where I can watch him sit eternally

dreaming over his typewriter?
then, at last, will I finally unlearn

everything? and I admit that yes,
while I could never leave

everyone, here at last
I understand these yellow flowers,

the names, the black door
he held open

and you walked through.

DEAR PINK FLOWER

what are you thinking
did you grow in a giant glass house
or some anonymous field
without admonition
maybe someone drove all night
or an unceremonious horn
announced the appearance
of a ship from the fog
full of you and others
packed in boxes
what are you thinking
still holding your pink
blossom tightly
in the protective green
leaves I'm sure have
a name but I don't
want to look at a screen
I just want to look
at you here
in this silent kitchen
implacably waiting
there is no detectable
death along your petals
yet that lighter shade
soon will come
all morning I have been restless
I know there is something
I have not yet done
I did not sew
the deep blue future

with silver thread
pink flower you are
the only one I can tell
today is her birthday
I don't even know
what to thank
so I will very gently
reach out my hand
and touch those green
fingers that finally
opened to hold
up your giant pink head
in futile gratitude
if it is all the same to you

THE DEATH POEMS OF
ULALUME GONZÁLEZ DE LEÓN

lots of poets
speak to the dead
or so they say
but who dies
on purpose
so she can speak
to the living
who gives
one last breath
back to the world
then stays
some time longer
to speak in the ear
of one who loved her
or maybe just us
her recorders
I don't know
whether ghosts feel
that's a subject
for the mystic
I am not
I want to know
what is past feeling
only for myself
a silver taste
appears in my mouth
so I drift away
to the pages
the death poems

I join them again
she spoke
one last time
into our ears
then without sentiment
went elsewhere

SUPREME DESPAIR SONG

On the morning of the decision
that feels like one more sign
we have come to the death
of everything not a lie
and only malevolence
can change anything
I do not want to imagine
I just want to look
outside just another day
another day of sunshine
and that mountain
I don't want to transform
with a single metaphor
and anger the gods
I wish would wake up
and get to smiting
or stay asleep long enough
for us to steal something
that will solve everything
what a childish wish
leave that for tomorrow
or never again
today I just want to look
and think and be quiet
and figure out how
things I do can matter
how I can keep dreaming
when I am awake
but not of a perfect world

YOGURT PARK

Sometimes I need to walk out

into the cool evening

and like the opposite

of a nearly dead from hunger

explorer go in an utterly

calm quest for

the artificial glory of a mountain

of what is surely frozen

imitation fake petroleum

loaded with little baby

mountains of ostensible

chocolate which all feels

sinfully iterative what is

the result I take

unnatural nature into

my body digitally

weep then turn away

away from everything

intelligent everything

edifying everything sweet

sweet and bitter

are my loves

how they beckon me

back from this mountain

of needless want

and how despite

the shadows I put

inside me back

to them I go

is the great subject

I avoid toward it I walk

gradually then suddenly

GOWN
for Dean Young

When I was so deep in my trouble
he sent me a jade skull

I looked at it every day
and felt its pale green
laugh

fill me and turn
into a few words

maybe the end
of a hymn

to the waitress who brought us
fake absinthe
that time
in a gown

he said she had an aura

I said I've never
seen one

we went home and fell asleep
but not forever

in the morning he shook me
gently and said

keep looking

FOR YOUNG POETS

People talk about flowers

all the time just like

they talk about nuns

and pianos but hardly

anyone can explain exactly

what they are for

how exactly they work

do they choose to go

into the cloister

and become a certain

hue the sun can pass

through attracting notes

that come from a wire

struck by a wooden hammer

or did they hear

a voice once or for many

years that said if you

focus all your love

on this single blade

that doesn't

feel anything something

will fly by and touch

your keys with powder

on its wings and make

music only you were

destined to hear

in the meadow when

you hear it stay there

and wait your calyx

will open it's true

when it does no

matter what they say

there will still be time

for just a little while

keep that music

for yourself

POEM FOR ROBERT DESNOS

you were born in a butcher shop
owned by your father an addled ghost
who might have also run a tavern
the tablets are unclear
the fly buzzed unhappily in the doorway
it wanted to tell the world
and the sun delayed setting for an hour
across the ocean it was Independence Day
and a new millennium saw the buffalo
dying out on the endless plains
no one in the Marais
knew the world had changed
everyone talked softly
about yesterday and poured
too much emerald liquid into glasses
beveled and reflecting the sea
though it was thousands of years away
caressing the stone docks of Marseille
and the flagstones bloomed
much further east the Black Madonna
with her miraculous powers
waited patiently for your arrival
the black geometry of her face
the gorgeous abstraction
of her scars as she holds the child
holding a box of unknown reliquaries
with her actual tears in the dark green forest
she saved Bright Mountain
now she cries only when she is alone
so no one but you can gather the liquid

full of tiny silver clouds
for now in the butcher shop
the baby sleeps and outside
under sinister chimneys wraiths
of knowledge walk toward the door

THUS

I don't know why
I keep thinking
of my first car,
so dark and green,
the perfect color
for disappearing
at night into the deep
park with its roads
that led to friends,
the mystery
of their kindness,
without a thought
I let them all go,
it was so old
but carried me
across the quadrate
capital where
I was born,
I drove through
shadows giant white
buildings cast,
sometimes spring
blossoms from famous
trees the mayor
of Tokyo gave us long
before the war
on my windshield
fell, one winter
when I was young
the radio told me
a plane crashed

into the bridge
then the DJ made
a terrible joke
and I laughed,
was that when
I began to snow,
a thousand years
of ice covered
my path, before
I ever found it
I lost even my
thought of home,
if from the provinces
I should return
I will drive
to the bridge,
stop and get out
wearing the black
luxurious coat
with a torn
lining my father
gave away,
touch the railing,
look down in the dark
the water contains
and wonder
where did
the bodies go,
will they pull them
out or wait
until spring,
what calculations,
are you still there

under the dark,
should I destroy
this mountain
of snow on my hand,
the buildings with
their vacancies
beckon but I must
stay here just a few
centuries longer,
who first told me
about that meadow
no one has found
without falling
asleep to forget
all the most
beloved ones,
terrible meadow
where I went
to be safe
from my only
ones who will
keep me safe,
how much longer
must I stay here
in this meadow
the blue bees visit,
to them all
flowers are strange,
they love no one
thus and thus
they do no harm.

TOURMALINE

is a stone some say
helps put a feverish child
to sleep

and others
claim it wakes actors
from the necessary
trance of illusion

to become themselves again

it comes in many colors
like the strange red
stone set into the Russian Imperial Crown
everyone thought
was the second-largest ruby

in the world
and maybe it is
but might be tourmaline
which would explain

certain dreams
of Catherine the Great

I love green
tourmaline the most

to look at it
is to become a leaf
falling
into a bottomless mirror

you look in
and see not yourself
but the final pure lake

you are falling toward

and the sun refuses to set
so you forget your face

and lie down
in the street with everyone
and stop everything

its green glow warm in your right hand

your ear pressed to the asphalt
listening for further instructions

SUNFLOWER POEM

I want to fall asleep
in the middle of the afternoon

but I stand here in the yard
wondering why I planted the sunflowers
yesterday all over the garden,

knowing they would never grow
nearly tall enough to penetrate
the diurnal gloom or turn

their heads to follow their lamp,

I've never planted anything
but a voice kept saying *now*,

so I went out
into the yard like someone
who wants the trees

to think he has a plan
and desperately strewed the seeds,

all afternoon the leaves like green coins
above my head
in the single redwood

my neighbors planted 60 years ago
so it is still young
made that sound,

and the old skull cloud came to complain
for too long about a handsome ice storm
that promised to return last winter,

the lamp softens all things it nears

soon I will go near it because I need
to write the difficult letter that says enough,

but first the skull says it was you
who planted these sunflowers
and now they are growing

far too tall, nothing
can support that golden weight,

go slip through the chipped green gate
to ask forgiveness of the forest,

some voice will answer
I was the one who came
to you and told you

put the seeds in the black soil then forget
the deeds of your enemies

you did one
and not the other and now
those sunflowers

will grow so tall their golden heads
will fall into the earth
and unlike you they will never die.

THE EVENING MEETING

finally the hour has come
it is time for the long journey
I say to my wife and child a last farewell

and click the blue button
my face appears across from my face
it is the day we will virtually discuss

the unpredictable resolutions I am sure
obscurely will decide my fate
the ostensible chair begins to speak

he says thank you for your electrons
I hope you are well in these days
or at least surviving

I touch the hem of a book
someone says that's a lot of togetherness
someone says the asymptote of dusk

the chair mutes us all
it's so good to see all your faces
thank you for availing

this interstitial convocation
to consider these extraordinary times
I put on my educator mask and stare

into the unsmiling grid
trying to look as if I understand
the one named after a star

she has mastered this new technology
she shares the document of potential paths
through the forest

into uncertain autumn
we talk and wander among them
we must decide but cannot stop

a great blanket of acknowledged despair
in the form of silence threatens until the one
with all the hidden power speaks

his eyeglasses catch the light
he says it is my sad role to remind you
that yes there are bodies piled in the streets

but don't forget the learning outcomes
then the most mordant of us utters
if I may quote my accountant

all solutions are suboptimal
laughter ripples through the proximate squares
for a moment we sit sensing

vital decisions
faces keep speaking
they dissolve and become

shapes on my screen
more and more they resemble
lonely ships

carrying protocols into the distance
the voices get further away
at last the endless meeting ends

into the dark screen I begin
to recite the ever more infinite list
of things I do not know

LA PLAGUE

The funniest thing that happened
in high school French was not me bringing
an elaborate bûche de Noël i.e. a Christmas cake
shaped like a log and covered
in chocolate whipped cream my parents
stayed up all night making
for my classmates who stared at what was
suddenly all too unmistakably
a massive poo I had to cut up
and hand to them one by one their faces
distorted in various attempts not to weep
nor when Lars inexplicably fell
out of his chair and shouted
in perfectly accented Spanish *mierda!*
nor the two weeks the substitute
sat buried in a romance novel
while I along with he who was forced
to be known as Pierre for his name
without gallic equivalent was Brendan
systematically threw
every Victor Hugo one by one
out of the back window onto the cars
parked in the teachers' lot and each time
they made the exact same most
objectively correlated immensely
satisfying thud yes those
astounding moments still
after 35 years shine but the best
was when Eric was asked naturellement
in French by the terrifying Mme. Kitzes

what he thought of the book
by Camus we were supposed to have read
all weekend instead of imagining
somewhere there was some party we almost
got invited to instead of with grim
determination masturbating to the soft
tones of Aztec Camera and he called it
La Plague instead of *La Peste*
which made it absolutely clear
that if he had considered reading
anything at all it was that little red book
in English we had somehow all
managed to procure and Mme. Kitzes
looked at him with absolute middle-aged
homicidal grief I have many times
felt myself now that I am what
the leaders of this webinar I currently
have the responsitunity to watch
call an educator and none of us could stop
laughing at ourselves which in those
holy wasted days was everything.

ALL APRIL

We stayed inside
and drew red trains

we ate burritos
like it was the end

the air was sweeter
for a good long while

everything had stopped
so many people we know

lost so much so fast
so many others

did not come and sit
near our door and say

how is your garden
your little sunflowers

they say are simple
to grow in a line

it is said their heads
turn to watch the sun

but they don't at all
no birds ever came

to eat the green shoots
my little sunflowers

I watched them poke up
through the soft black dirt

with that undeserved pride
I feel when he writes his name

I did not teach him guitar
like I was my dad

I just put him in the car
and played the Beatles

and drove back and forth
through his favorite tunnel

it got dark and light
then so dark again

SUNDAYS

it's sad how I'm so proud
of how carefully I dug

my finger in the black earth
to make a little space for something

to come up from the ground
and now I can't stop thinking

those crows in the trees
why are they so terrible

they seem like one big eye
trained on my little green shoots

because of those few seeds
I am now an arbiter

I decide which natural beings
must by means of loops

of wire be defeated and starve
while I watch over my green towers

why must I think of this garden
as the insoluble problem

of inherent sadness
that same song tires me

I just don't like the way it sounds
dirt doesn't need to be written about

let's water my actual protoflowers
then go to the dream of the park

and play hello goodbye
then do you hear the crow

look up it's another terrible Sunday
hours and hours of space

to experience doing something
without leaving

the tree above our heads
doesn't protect anything

it really does seem to be not
promising but breathing

THE SUPER BOWL

Everyone knows Kansas
is flatter than any other state
except for Mount Sunflower,
which rises in triumphant
anonymity. The plains admire
its noble arrogance, it is
always victorious over
everything no matter
the challenges. Everyone
knows Sundays are for
sleeping through the news.
Everyone knows the handsome
son of America will win,
but they are both so full
of beef authority it is
impossible to tell them apart,
especially in their armored
vulnerability. Everyone knows
one is older, he lives
like a lion unretired
in the sleepy mysteries
of the state that dangles
into the sea. What does
he eat? No one knows. The sea
is the Atlantic, it is so cold,
every night he swims
in it and starlight
caresses his form. Everyone
knows this year the color
red will win and we will all

clean up salty triangular
vehicles for conveying
variegated deliciousness,
we cannot stop, our
hands are alive, everyone
knows it will all end
and we will start talking
about how long it feels until
we can sit together again
and watch big men
fight off pretend death.
Everyone knows one
will fall and the other
will stand over his body, weeping.
Then they will present him
with the bowl, indeed
you can fill it with anything
and it will never overflow.
Everyone knows
a horse takes three hours
to gallop from one end
of the Grand Canyon
to the river to touch
its nose to the red stone.

GENTLE DEATH POEM

is what I had written in my sleep

with that hand that belongs to no one

I wish I could remember that world

it probably had some birds in it

alien punctuation marks

clarifying the sky

here in this one

we stare and stare

a blank grey that is basically

a color that isn't even one

bouncing off the leaves in the yard

making everything lunar

my waking hand doesn't believe

my dream hand

it says death can be gentle

I'm out of time to argue

it's easier just to stay

inside the idea that I get to choose

which one of us will go first

and which one will stay

here to take care of the little leaf

that fell into our house and now hides

from the darkness of the actual

from the wind's eternal certainty

POEM FOR WITOLD GOMBROWICZ

I'm reading your diary
is a weird thing to say
even to someone dead
who lived in Argentina,
furious at Europe
for all its museums
full of poor people crying
for the amusement of strangers,
I can vacuum all day
and the book will be waiting,
open all the wrong doors
and your voice will be there
saying poets are enemies
of anything real,
poets think flowers
love them
and every pastry
deserves an elegy,
I took a train to Poland
and breathed in
so much black smoke
near to the odd rust-colored
monument to your birth
made of local stone,
the train hurtled through
vast forests whose names
sound like monsters,
I took so many notes
about vital matters
of the heart and mind,

it's a kind of discipline
not to remember
who I was in the past,
I hoard all my energy
for future atoning,
on your birthday
to honor you
I will pull down my trousers
with total disrespect
and pee on a very old tree.

I SEE YOU

You built the blue
chair out of blue

pieces from
a box we turned

into a ship
that lifted toward

then past
the rings of Saturn

into the void
that waited for him

full of friends
far from the sun

he loves Pluto
so much we hid

the sad news
of its recent demotion

you bent down
and held the drill

your hair hung
down in that dangerous

proximity they warn
us in the instructions

must be avoided
and all was well

then you called
the man who is

known as father
and took it in

his endless worry
that might be love

then you filled
the bath with tears

laughing with me
at our ridiculous fear

of the Lego
of the dangerous future

then we sat
in the chair together

I placed my foot
on your foot

no one was lost
no one watched us

watch the sunflowers
grow a little

as the sun went
where it goes

no one watched
us watch them grow

MY PHONES

I remember when I got my first
I plugged it in and left it carefully
in my apartment then went to the bar
my friend the lawyer laughed at me
soon without a thought I learned to carry
a little black portal and look down
the instant I disenthralled the world
it seemed some contract was always ending
giving me a chance to go to the store
and sign another few years away
I liked each new one in my hand
holding it probably helped me stop smoking
so I could live longer and use more
of those minutes I worried and forgot about
for a while that was how they monetized time
until it revealed itself as pure attention
and like you I became the permanent
unpaid intern to that beautiful word *silicon*
I sat with it once to my ear in a rest stop
a few hours outside of Chicago
through it I heard my father tell me
some news about a small dot in his brain
that didn't matter then like everyone
I recognized fate could see me too
now I look at the map and know
I am one of those 60 billion green pings
moving through Central Park or the Pentagon
like you I beam my harmless location
in case I lose it my expensive window
I think I am the one who looks through
unwilling not to be found

THE LAST POEM
for Sarah

The last poem I will ever write
will be like the first one I ever

wrote down, when I was green like a lawn
that did not know it was not the world,

I had gone to school and learned to be
a little angry argument machine

and all the dittos slept in the blue
light of filmstrips about the last war,

and we stood in line for the movie
about robots who saved everything

with the help of people that taught them
the essential importance of death,

words they did not need to understand
but only speak when they faced the gate,

then I went home and read the stories
about Norse gods and fell into sleep

with its unrealistic drawings
and never woke up until we met

and this was what I remembered
from a sleep that told me not

what was but what would be:
Mother and Father standing there,

each wearing the faces of those ones
whose benevolence cannot be changed

by actions or time, they are constant
like a room that hides in an old book

you filled with wildflowers and sunlight.

TRAINS IN JAPAN

go so smoothly
through forests and towns

three types of pine
a few needles fall

the trees have adapted
the city doesn't notice

hundreds of millions
of beings each with silent

essays moving
through their minds

like orange fish
with spots of gleaming lacquer

along the perimeter
of a black rectangular

pond in the museum
the silver train passes

no longer the fastest
in the world

it enters the city
the gleaming future

doesn't notice
I want to go

with my son there
so he can draw them

we will sit at a station
where they can see us

being harmless
we make plans

the trees laugh
those dark magistrates

examine the palindrome
of the reactor

a light rain falls
on the memorial

to the world

THE ELEGANT TROGON

The South American trogon
is a gentle bird with weak legs
and soft colorful feathers.
It nibbles holes in trees
to make its nest. One flew
into my sleep and dropped
a golden tooth into my supinated
hand, then perched croaking
on a twig. It appeared
to be wearing spectacles.
Special effects, said an Eastern
Elusive Spadefoot Toad,
digging calmly as a scholar
of the Era of Good Feelings.
I felt a rictus travel across
my face, arriving at my mouth
in the form of an effortful
grimace. Dawn was carrying
something quantum in its oral
cavity and purring. I have
a secret pigeon in my heart.
I keep it in a cage composed
of object lessons and feed it
moral law. Every morning
it stirs and wakes me with
its lonely cooing and together
we wander into a sort of
guilty state of already feeling
as if we are at loggerheads
with the turtle of doing what

we ought to do. Now I am
fully awake. Still I feel that golden
lodestone burning in my palm.
Which I plan on keeping locked.

I DREAM OF LEON SPINKS

In my dream
as he did in life
he raises his arms
and we are all
alive in 1978,
sitting uneasily
as always too
close together
on the green couch,
watching the soon
to be defeated
greatest one
rest against
the ropes,
time didn't need
his gorgeous sneer
to touch the canvas
to instruct us
no glorious failure
awaits, you just
watch the most
beautiful man
who ever lived
await the judges,
already defeated
his eyes
absently fix
on some distant
grey room beyond
all possibility, then

the black numbers
on the cards
appear to tell him
what he knew,
my father said
go to bed
and never forget
the gold belt
only pauses
in your hands,
so we went
and put our heads
on the soft stair
that leads down
beyond the past
and slept and
slept and did not
know the old
cruelties had just
dissolved
into new ones
or that trucks
were already moving
toward the city
to wait not so
many years
for that very
temporary champion
to unload them
in the snow.

THE EMPTY GRAVE OF
ZSA ZSA GABOR

On the radio I heard
that inimitable accent
say I vant to die
where I was born,
I remember her
so long ago
appearing on certain
Saturday nights
as I religiously wasted
my youth watching
others embark
the boat of love,
rogues and ingenues
disappeared into
commercial breaks
unravaged then
into buffet light
emerged dazed
with a contentment
I have never felt,
some nights
she stepped
off the gangplank
so gracefully
stumbling a little,
one hand stretched
out to the dashing
purser, the other
holding the million

dollar nickel
of always about
to escape without
becoming a bride,
sometimes clad
in the white fur
attitude of a girl
from the Kremlin
who wouldn't talk
to one untouched
by evil, at others
under a blue hat,
a countess of
what could have been
were I not who I was,
she also appeared
perched amid
the luminous
Hollywood square
of afternoons
pretending not
to know facts
about outer space
or islands or headless
queens, her laughter
a sentient bell,
and never was
she until those last
days in the hospital
allowed to be
alone, then one
afternoon just as

she wished
her soul left
the body we all
desired and returned
to the old land,
wind came looking
but could not find her.

THE BLUES BAND

The waitress told us it was going to get busy
in town again,

the blues band was coming
and I felt that familiar ancient sorrow
since childhood

of remembering some people
are actually able
to take pleasure
in belonging,

though it is true I have actually attended campfires, dark
water crashed in the darkness,

we felt the pleasure
of pure young sorrow, adoring without being adored,

far from here
the sea crashes
but even the darkness

of forgetting cannot obliterate
what seem to be the most tender
sounds made

by those I have forgotten, they are
only shapes to me now,
maybe they are still there, in the sunlit
sorrow of former farmers markets
where vacant vegans once

chunkled away at various instruments,
an unexamined tendency to sentimentalize
the East and its lessons about freedom
from the self
emerges in the form
of a wandering melody,

that's your former PE teacher playing
the sax with enviable abandon, what
were once electric cries of rage and sorrow

dissipating in their interpretation,
here, so far

inland already the first chords
are audible from the future, coming closer,

at last they have arrived to regiment
us all into the army

of fun, I'm not
against fun, per se, not everything
has to be sorrow, but it seems

some songs
never end, they just pause in a clatter

of repressed sorrow and then resume
elsewhere, certain body parts that should
have remained
unshaken shake, and yes

I know, who am I to say
what is blue, what is true sorrow,
let America have its fun,

shaking while the ghost of sorrow
among us
walks, unamused.

POEM BEGINNING WITH A LINE
BY JIMÉNEZ

like the sea on the telephone
I call you from the other room

you are a blue iceberg
of unwavering attention

you have your headphones on
as if for however long

you keep listening whatever
can harm us will pass us by

your handsome thief
is happily sleeping his friend

my subaltern is in the forest
he stumbles into a cave

holding the stolen vase
out from his body

instead of a light
for an instant there's a little glow

and we see the paintings
delicate aurochs

with alien eyes
graze at the feet of the beings

known only through their mounds
full of fine tools

we still can't believe they made
they were formed

with perfect precision
we don't know how to use them

when touched those objects
send out a chime

in the direction of a particular star
that if we are still here

will bring our doom
in a great cavern my subaltern stands

the sound he hears
at the foot of a lake

is where water meets the wind
and he knows his fate is elsewhere

he carefully places the vase
back among the stalagmites

and begins the long journey back
to the land of uneasy

beautiful agreements
he must hurry there is something

he must tell us
I want to call out to you again

but my mouth will not open

HVAR

On the day I left, it was nearly silent,
just wind through the white buildings,
a few grandmothers talking.

I had gone there instead of another place,
was I not alone?

I was but someone was with me.
I look at the picture now, I had forgotten.
Just a slight shadow
also disembarking.

Now the hotel
and everything
that happened there is gone

though the path through the lavender
to the square, surprisingly large,
with its many tables,
and the little stone staircase

all the way on the other side,
almost invisible

that went up to the shop where they sold
leather goods, the brown smooth
sandals people wear

even after they go back to the city,
still wait.

I tried to be happy
with myself in my notebook,
I sat awkwardly by the water,
drinking bitter coffee
from comically small cups.

I was there, so I rode off
brave as a motorbike
through the wild mountains

into an abandoned town
where I left nothing for
the people who will come to build
everything again,

maybe they've found
a good life high on that hill
now that the war is over.

On the day I left
the market was silent
waiting for holy bells,
the nearby crashing waves,
a form getting onto a boat,

it was me, I was leaving,
and I knew I would never

remember something I learned
when I walked away
and said

I will not stop
trying to return

to the path of silent lavender,
the steps that lead into the water.

LISTENING TO PAINTINGS

for Shirley Cookston, Diego Rivera, and Joan Mitchell

Diego, at last I am sitting
before your giant

painting of everything.
Since you left

it's been so dark,
we don't even know

what is information anymore.
Finally we are emerging

into the bright museum.
It may even be good

that everything is different,
and also to think

all the time about breathing.
To sit on benches

and imagine
those just like us

nearly a century ago
were afraid of different things.

It was just before we entered
another great war. They sat

in an airplane hangar
and watched you paint

this mural. I wonder if
they were amazed

you could so exactly place
on the faces of strangers

such familiar expressions,
as if their lost

sisters and brothers
once more stood

before them looking
in other directions.

In the center you painted
a huge machine. It faces us

like a constructed god.
On one side I see a wheel,

on the other a giant
hand raised in a position

that could be a greeting
or warning. On its

brown skin are four
turquoise dots. I feel

almost sure I know
what they mean.

Your analog mirror
built to listen to the future

foresaw many things,
but how could you

have imagined
we worry rain

at all the wrong times
means that we have punched

a hole in the sky,
is not even close

to our biggest problem.
I don't know why you put Frida

in the center standing
painless as a spire, leaving

out her wounded spine.
Maybe you knew we will always

be too young for the truth.
You touched the painting

one last time,
made a little bow

then departed forever
like the final dream

of unity from our skulls.
I just sit for a while

here at the bottom of the stairs
until I am called

upward to other rooms
softly exploding

with the modern.
There familiar colors

seem brighter. Joan
your paintings are correct,

each friend bewilders
in the most necessary

ways, each one
flickering

like magenta
overseeing a small

private body of water,
each a master

of some essential blue.
When I stand here

I really do believe
I have always been

toward your paintings
journeying. The longer

I travel the longer
the trip. Sometimes

I arrive in a smear
of lemon, a little

dream plane,
then keep going

to wake again
alive inside the question

of my life, one
you keep

with your colors
asking: geometrically

complex feelings,
how shall I

make them known?

THE EMPATHY MUSEUM
for Matt Small

I have never seen

a face in a painting

that made me wonder

more what happens

at night when

the gallery

is locked

all the apertures

to the world

are closed

so now

with eyes still open

the painting stares

into the room

no longer

is the painting

mistaken

for a mirror

in which we believe

we see the same

almost nameable

feelings which arise

in us too

now that we're gone

a little glow

from afar

maybe the end

of dead galaxies

or a streetlight

whose light

the word *ancient*

cannot begin

to describe

with total disinterest

touches the eyes

at last the museum

has become

a museum of empathy

at last the face

is where it belongs

FAILED ELEGY

It seems these days
every poem is a failed elegy

for the world. Each one
asks correctly, what good

did writing this do? I cannot
deny I often feel anger

at the similarities between me
and an oil company, especially

on what is once again
the hottest day ever recorded.

It is so easy to do nothing
except lament our success

at writing useless laments.
I must confess I too

once wrote a ridiculous elegy
for a broken nail clipper.

I said it caught the light
of a distant star where beings

look down on us, disappointed
yet hopeful we will, like poets,

put things in the right order
just in time. The clipper

emitted a confusing, not very
mysterious blue light. Sometimes

it seems to me the job of a poet
is mostly to rearrange the deck chairs

next to a perfect blue
swimming pool, then in those

chairs to doze. In another failed
elegy I described how all day

we walked through mist to get
to the exact spot where Dean specified

we should disperse his ashes.
It was windy, and we got a lot of him

on our hands. In the poem I wrote
he shares the name of a chef

at Infinity Hospital, which sounds
like but is not a beautiful lie.

Then I wrote, when I imagine how
he must have felt to try to write

poems with a new heart
he got from someone younger

who died, I feel mine
fill with the echo of replacement,

which was not exactly or perhaps
too true. The truth is I walked

along through the mist thinking
many boring things, not feeling

like much of anything except
stopping. We walked

through a field of wildflowers
that left some yellow powder

on our shoes. I just wanted
to be home with my wife and son,

but the mist really did seem endless.
Unlike death, it was not. We drove

slowly through the little town
until we found a place to eat

and did not speak of death.
Speaking of speaking of death,

Emily Dickinson compared herself
to the little wren because she knew

it was small and unremarkable.
It sings the most notes and sometimes

will take a ride for a little while
to eternity in the overcoat

of a passing stranger.

I DON'T KNOW

the little candle
in front of the portrait
of your mother

flickers with happiness
a river of years
flows past your sleeping
lonely form

every morning
the anxious quiet
unhelpful phantoms
say to me
you have forgotten

what feeling
is surrounded by glass
inside the museum of
not knowing

and what the dog
is barking at

and why just now
I felt sure
ghosts caress
the infirmary

and where snow starts
I mean at what point it's snow

and who told me the thing
that controls what I do
what that thing is
where is it

I hear them
while I am wandering

through the part
of morning
just before
everything explodes

the little candle
quiet and anxious
on its own
just went out

then started reaching
for something again

ACKNOWLEDGMENTS

My thanks to the editors of the following publications, where these poems first appeared:

"Failed Elegy," *The Atlantic*

"My Grandmother's Dictionary," *The New Yorker*

"Poem for a Suicide," *Poem-a-Day*

"Thoughts on Punctuation," "Tell Me Why," "Bad Bear," "Dead Flowers," "The Locksmith," *The American Poetry Review*

"Peoria," *Air/Light*

"The Evening Meeting," *The Paris Review*

"Sunflower Poem," *Alta*

"All April," "The Last Poem," "Listening to Paintings," *Harvard Review*

"Sundays," *Indiana Review*

"Gentle Death Poem," "Poem for Witold Gombrowicz," *Iterant*

"I See You," *jubilat*

"My Phones," *The New York Times*

"Poem for Rupi Kaur," *Together in a Sudden Strangeness*, edited by Alice Quinn (Alfred A. Knopf, 2020)

"I Dream of Leon Spinks," *Rosebud*

"The Empty Grave of Zsa Zsa Gabor," *A Public Space*

"Hvar," *Poetry London*

"The Super Bowl," "The Blues Band," *Alaska Quarterly Review*

"Poem for Jean Follain," "I Love Hearing Your Dreams," "I Don't Know," "Poem Beginning with a Line by Jiménez," *Jung Journal*

"Trains in Japan," *The Shanghai Literary Review*

"The Empathy Museum," *Reverberations*

"It Was Summer. The Wind Blew," *You Are Here: Poetry in the Natural World*, edited and introduced by Ada Limón (Milkweed Editions, 2024)

"Gown," *The Threepenny Review*

"Tourmaline," *The Paris Review*

NOTES

In "Poem Beginning with a Line by Jiménez," "like the sea on the telephone" ("como el mar en teléfono") is a line from Juan Ramón Jiménez's 1916 poem "Hacia el mar (Diario de un poeta recién casado)," "Toward the Sea (Diary of a Newlywed Poet)."